A Walk On
The Moor

A Walk On The Moor

POEMS BY
COLIN COX

THE CHOIR PRESS

First published in the United Kingdom in 2018 by
The Choir Press

ISBN 978-1-911589-63-1

Acknowledgements:
Some of these poems have appeared before in Poetry Now Home Counties Anthology 1996, and Poetry Now 'The Sweetest Thing' Anthology 1997.

I would like to thank Eleanor Pollard for her great help with bringing this book to fruition and also Ken Rowland for his input in the initial stages.

Cover photograph by
Daniel J Rao/Shutterstock.com

For Dorothy

Contents

Writing A Poem

I always think
when I sit down
to write a poem
that it will come

tumbling out with
form and content
finely crafted.

Reality
disillusions.

If You Were Not Here

If you were not here
gone over to there
what freedom each night
to do as I like.

But I would soon miss
that sweet tender kiss
that love which endures
and gently immures.

So I'd send my plea
please come back to me,
and I'll never again
of constraining complain.

Playing With Hannah (Aged 4¼)

'Grandad. I'll stay here,
and you stay over there.
Now I'll throw the ball
against the garden wall,
and see who can catch it fast
before it bounces on the grass.'

'Grandad. Play night times with me, and keep
very very quiet while I cover you up to sleep.
I'll shout you when it's morning.
Get up Grandad. It's morning! morning!'
'But I've only just gone to bed.'
'Well it's morning so do what I said!'

'Hannah you're very bossy.' 'No I'm not!'
Hannah smiles a little, then a lot.
'It's time for bed again. I'll cover you up.'
'But I've just *been* to bed, and I've only just got up'
'Grandad! Do as you're told
or I won't play with you again until you're very old!'

The Mermaid

A beauty bared
all glistening black
resting alone
on storm forged rock.

Her skin feels so smooth,
yet cold to the touch.
She smells of the sea,
and silently sits

with charm and allure
enticing young salts
to watery graves.

An Ordinary Life

Life for many can be rather mundane,
and not in any way full of pain
or dangerous or fearful,
but in many ways uneventful.

Though some might say this type of experience
is boring, even a burden in a sense,
it seems to me a cause for celebration
when considering how much aggravation
can be heaped upon the ordinary man
by the vicissitudes of life's span.

Sweet And Sour

How sweet! That pair of robins in the sun.
We've watched them work so hard to build their nest.
And now, with grubs, they've fed and filled their young
they've stopped to take a well-earned rest.

Two birds aghast and overcome with grief
as wily cat with stealth completes his quest.
And there, before their helpless gaze, the thief
plucks all four fledglings from that cherished nest.

The true significance
of that idyllic scene!
We watched as in a trance
while nature crushed our dream.

Love's Promise

Lying next to me warm and sleeping
with breasts softly rising and falling
as I awake I find you still
there once again that beautiful girl.

Such loveliness! But how can it be
that you should want to lie here with me?
Do you not see my many faults
the mistakes, the weaknesses, those naughts?

Or if you see, as so surely you must,
then why stay with me to care for and fuss?
It can only be love which blinds you
and excuses those things that I do.

When you waken I'll make amends, and please
that I be worthy of this love which sees
only the bold brave man that I would be,
and not the one who tries yet is not he.

The Ancient Redwood Tree

Though you may be
a mighty tree
don't think you're free
to lord it over me.

You may have seen
my forebears' births,
and later seen
them live, then leave this earth,

yet take good care
to treat with me
showing respect
and due humility.

Else though it's true
you've seen me child and man
you'll not survive that long
to see me through life's span.

For soon I might
return with axe and saw
to show you what is meant
by pride before a fall.

Sometimes

Sometimes it rains,
but then grey gives way to blue,
and jewelled raindrops sparkle
as bird songs start anew.

Sometimes it's dark,
but however deep the night
inexorably it yields
to the glimpse of days first light.

Sometimes sadness reigns,
but it cannot stay immune
to smiles, infectious laughs
which cheer, and lift the gloom.

Sometimes death stalks our path,
but though we shiver as he passes by,
yet are we warmed, enveloped by that sound:
a baby's cry!

I Know When You're There
(Message from a Nursing Home in Weston Super Mare)

Though you think I'm gaga
with my vacant stare
I do have my thoughts,
and I do know when you're there.

I may need some help to walk,
but once I'm in my chair
I'm happy with my lot,
and I do know when you're there.

Sorry my estate declines
to pay for all this care,
but my thoughts are with you,
and I do know when you're there.

Though you may write me off,
'He doesn't know us when we're there',
don't forget it could be you
sitting in this chair.

So will you come today
to Weston Super Mare?
For though think I'm gaga
with my vacant stare
I do have my thoughts,
and I do know when you're there.

Me

I am lucky to have:
    A brain which functions normally,
    as far as I know.
    Eyes that see.
    A heart which has not faltered, yet.
    Lungs to oxygenate my blood.
    Hands to feel and hold with.
    Feet which carry my weight.
    An ordinary personality.
    A socially acceptable face.

And, above all, I am lucky to be:
    Just me.

Last Chocolates

Chocolate is more seductive
than all the foods I know.
I can't resist its lure
especially when I'm low.

Though I resolve to change and diet
my will is weak and cheats:
as I seek solace once again
amongst my chocolate treats.

I try to hide with flowing dresses
my figure once my pride,
and when I'm asked my weight I laugh,
but die a bit inside.

I dream that I'm a youthful figure
of grace and beauty rare,
but when I wake and face the truth
how deep is my despair.

So can I change and diet?
Be that female of my dreams?
Yes! As soon as I have eaten
just one more box of chocolate creams.

Miss Eleanor Faith Pollard
(Born 11.00pm 23rd April 1996)

How can it be that I'm now me
Miss Eleanor Faith P?
Yesterday I lay nestled inside my Mum,
but, this evening at eleven, I've just begun
to find out what it's like to be
a thing apart: a separate entity.

And what a shock and trauma at my birth.
With all that pushing I thought that I must burst
until, expelled naked into this great big world,
I lay there cold, exposed. Oh how my senses whirled!

But now twelve hours have passed,
and I am learning very fast
that in this bright and noisy world I'm in
it's sometimes me who's making all the din.
And that when the lights seem far too bright
it's not so bad if I shut my eyes up very tight.
And that if I lay quiet and fall asleep I'm back,
in my dreams, safely wrapped in my amniotic sac.

And now two days have passed,
and, though I'm learning very fast,
I still can't understand why
I have to wait so long for food I cry.
Don't they know I'm used to having nourishment poured
constantly in through my umbilical cord?

And now a week has passed,
and, though I'm learning very fast,
I still can't understand why
they don't know that when I cry,
instead of sleeping in my cot,
it's because I'm cold or sometimes very hot.
Don't they know that before I was a separate me
my temperature was always kept at thirty seven degrees C?

And now a month has passed,
and I'm still learning very fast
that if things aren't to my liking
all I need to do is start yelling
and, as if by magic, what I want will come.
Or, if they get it wrong, I yell again for Dad or Mum.
But in the end they seem to get it right
so I think I'm going to be fine both day and night.

Tom

The school say Tom's turned wild.
He's rude and runs about.
And if he does not get his way
he starts to stamp and shout.

Our neighbours say the same.
Their gardens they'd enjoyed,
but Tom's so trampled over them
that now they've been destroyed.

How can all this be true?
We cannot understand
when all the time we dote on him
and yield to each demand.

Whatever wants he has
we never would refuse,
and let him have his way with us
no matter what our views.

Whatever food he likes
we always try to find
from ice cream, biscuits, cakes and sweets
to crisps: the crinkly kind.

Whatever drinks he wants
we always give to him
from orange squash to alcopops,
and even drams of gin.

He knows that after work
we're far too tired to play,
but knows that he can surf the net
at will by night or day.

They say our Tom's turned wild,
but we don't understand
when all the time we dote on him
and yield to each demand.

The Garden Pond

When stresses crowding in
disturbed the inner me
I left the house and sat
beneath the aspen tree.

There, at the water's edge,
I saw so many creatures
weaving, darting, diving
amongst those aqueous features.

As I sat there dreaming
I joined the minnow shoal
glinting silver, turning,
into that gaping hole.

Then later, on my own,
I swam with pure delight,
but this great fish passed by
and caught me in his sight.

He chased me to exhaustion,
and, though I tried to hide,
he trapped me in the reed bed
teeth ripping down my side.

I woke up in an instant,
relieved that I was free,
those stresses in perspective
restored the inner me.

If I Had Met You Then

If I had met you then,
before we turned so grey,
what fun we could have had
when we were young and gay.

Now time has had its way
for going out to walk
is hard with aches and pains
so we just sit and talk.

And being old and wise
it's fun to reminisce
so no regrets remain
for youthful times we missed.

Unfulfilled Ambitions

What happened to all my youthful ambitions
of having riches and envied possessions?
Why did I not realise when
in former years I dreamt of them,
what toll the act of life itself
would wreak upon my visions?

The One You Seek

I love those pretty corners on the coast
or anywhere that I can see the sea.
But there I tend to wander like a ghost
without a friend to come along with me.

I like to go for walks in country lanes.
And, though my dog is sad if he's denied,
without a human friend my keenness wanes:
a friend to share my love of countryside.

I'm sure I go for meals to places you
would like as much as where you always dine.
It would be nice to go with someone who
like you appreciates good food and wine.

I read the advert that you placed this week,
and I feel sure that I'm the one you seek.

> **FEMALE** early forties, slim, attractive, enjoys
> seaside, countryside, gourmet meals out.
> Looking for male to share life with.

Storm Clouds In The Bay

Please don't go out to sea today;
no farewell kiss or fond goodbye,
while storm clouds gather in the bay.

While many mock I sit, and pray
that you will heed me when I cry
please don't go out to sea today.

I don't care what my sisters say,
how with the wind their menfolk fly,
while storm clouds gather in the bay.

The village children pause at play,
and wonder why I rage, and sigh
please don't go out to sea today.

The crones hold fast their tongues. For they
remember men who left to die
when storm clouds gathered in the bay.

For one last time don't sail away,
and leave me here alone to cry.
Please don't go out to sea today,
while storm clouds gather in the bay.

My Friend

Without really looking at
her well known rounded shape
I hold her again,
her comforting familiarity
of contoured smoothness
gently reassuring.

Sometimes my fingers burn
when her temperature rises.
Or else when very cold
only gloves can protect me
from her icy presence.

Life and death decisions
are made when holding her,
and I trust her implicitly
to be responsive to my touch;

my friend, who never makes
a sound, is always there
waiting for me, inert,
as I slide in
behind her each day:
my steering wheel.

A Walk On The Moor

As I set out upon the moor
this bright autumnal day
my cares familiar places pale,
and slowly fade away.

The grass is springy under foot,
and I am lifted high
by hearing lilting skylarks songs
within the clear blue sky.

Where later on I take a rest
a stream goes on its way,
and there I revel in the fun
of otters at their play.

Now I am deep within the moor,
and tired of being lone,
I see far off an angry sky
so quickly turn for home.

But dark ebullient clouds build up,
and soon the sun blank out.
So I've not travelled far and find
the storm is all about.

Above the threatening blackness mocks.
It knows there is no sanctuary,
and I'll be at its every whim
whatever it may do with me.

Large drops of rain begin to fall
each briefly held up on the turf,
and glistening in the fading light
then yielding to the pull of earth.

Though I try hard to keep my cheer
it starts again to pour and pour.
I feel a sense of gloom descend
as I am soaked, and soaked through more.

The rain now stops. My spirits rise.
But up above me, as before,
that evil blackness still stares down.
Alone I shiver on the moor.

While thunder rumbles overhead
a breeze, which soon turns blustery,
becomes a piercing icy blast
with hailstones lashing down on me.

As tiny grains of ice enlarge
a great accreted icy stone
strikes at my head and splits the skin.
'Leave me be!' I groan.

Above me in that black storm's heart
the clouds swirl violently together.
They form, cascade, divide, collide,
while building up its static pressure.

With wind increasing to a gale
the rain returns in force to form
torrential, horizontal sheets
thrust at me fiercely by the storm.

I am thrown down hard upon the sward
I rise up then stumble round and blunder
as that pent up force above explodes,
and the boiling sky is split asunder.

The loosed lightning streaks towards the ground
with a mighty crashing thunderous roar.
It angrily tears the air apart
exposing each tortured atom's core.

My poor body, racked with fear and awe,
lies prostrate before those heavens aroused
as the lightning strikes each hillock there,
and singes the turf before it's doused.

'Please no more' I cry, but there's no quarter.
It seems 'I' stand for the human race
within this so vain unequal struggle
with nature's primeval savage face.

In searching for the weakest of links
again once more a lightning point strike
which cracks and crashes down to the earth
to vent on me its venom and spite.

And now I can withstand it no more,
and lie here like a quivering leaf,
beneath this hate for man and his works,
a great oblivion gives me relief.

In my sleep I shout out and awake.
Am I truly at home in my bed?
Was it I on the moor in a storm
or a part of a dream full of dread?

It must have been a nightmare
that's soaked me through with sweat.
But no! See there! My pillow,
my blood's made red and wet!

Woodgrain

What a constant puzzle to me
is the pattern made by a tree
every time it's been converted
to a table, bench or workshed.

Those lines so close here,
yet far apart there.
Those circles or knots,
and ovals with tops.

What does it all mean?
There can not have been,
it's certain to me,
such lines in the tree.

But if tables and benches and worksheds could be
reassembled somehow back again to a tree
then how simple the puzzle's solution would be.

Your Bracelet

As I sort out your things
there it is, nestled
in that velvet green:
those golden tributes
to life's smiles of fortune
jumbled all together.

I count along the chain,
and there at number six
I stand too, hand in hand with you,
within the wedding ring.
After the day of your birth
marked in that engraving held
within the ambit of that golden Liver bird;
after my troth was pledged
with that diamond gleaming bright;
after your wayward flight
across the sea to follow me
in that noble glinting jet;
after your arrival in the land
of that lustrous maple leaf;
then were we two wed
in a great and joyous union.

But now my vision blurs
so afflicted by those memories' tears
that I can no longer see
those many gifts we shared
further down the chain
before the present's pain.

Now it's your turn to wait for me
as I waited then for you.
And when that joyful time arrives
that we're once more together
to celebrate we'll fashion
a celestial treasure
to fasten to the chain.

www.ingramcontent.com/pod-product-compliance
Lightning Source LLC
Chambersburg PA
CBHW040414110426
42813CB00013B/2649